HAMMERHEAD SHARK FILES

by Noah Leatherland

BEARPORT
PUBLISHING

Minneapolis, Minnesota

Credits
Images are courtesy of Shutterstock.com. With thanks to Getty Images, Thinkstock Photo, and iStockphoto. Recurring images – schab, nabil refaat, Maquiladora, A.Aruno. Cover – hvostik, Martin Voeller. 4–5 – Derek Heasley, EDGAR PHOTOSAPIENS. 6–7 – Martin Voeller, Vladislav Klimin. 8–9 – frantisekhojdysz, Martin Voeller. 10–11 – Joe Dordo Brnobic, frantisekhojdysz. 12–13 – Martin Prochazkacz, Ethan Daniels. 14–15 – Alex Rush, Matt9122. 16–17 – WorldTHROUGHme, Kristina Vackova. 18–19 – Paul Winkworth, FtLaudGirl. 20–21 – Steve Hinczynski, Tomas Kotouc. 22–23 – Natalya Chernyavskaya, Tomas Kotouc.

Bearport Publishing Company Product Development Team
President: Jen Jenson; Director of Product Development: Spencer Brinker; Managing Editor: Allison Juda; Associate Editor: Naomi Reich; Associate Editor: Tiana Tran; Art Director: Colin O'Dea; Designer: Kim Jones; Designer: Kayla Eggert; Product Development Assistant: Owen Hamlin

Library of Congress Cataloging-in-Publication Data is available at www.loc.gov or upon request from the publisher.

ISBN: 979-8-89232-062-7 (hardcover)
ISBN: 979-8-89232-536-3 (paperback)
ISBN: 979-8-89232-195-2 (ebook)

© 2025 BookLife Publishing
This edition is published by arrangement with BookLife Publishing.

North American adaptations © 2025 Bearport Publishing Company. All rights reserved. No part of this publication may be reproduced in whole or in part, stored in any retrieval system, or transmitted in any form or by any means, electronic, mechanical, photocopying, recording, or otherwise, without written permission from the publisher. Bearport Publishing is a division of Chrysalis Education Group.

For more information, write to Bearport Publishing, 5357 Penn Avenue South, Minneapolis, MN 55419.

CONTENTS

The Hammerhead Shark......4
Diet......................6
Mouth 8
Nose 10
Eyes 12
Skin.....................14
Skeleton 16
Fins 18
Tail 20
Life Cycle 22
Glossary 24
Index...................24

THE HAMMERHEAD SHARK

There are more than 500 kinds of sharks. The shape of the hammerhead shark's head sets it apart.

There are 10 kinds of hammerhead sharks. The smallest is only 35 inches (90 cm) long. The biggest can grow to be about 20 feet (6 m) long!

DIET

Hammerhead sharks are **predators**. Sometimes, they use their wide heads to hold down **prey** before taking a bite.

Smaller hammerhead sharks munch on small prey and sometimes even plants. Larger hammerheads hunt bigger animals, such as squids and stingrays.

A STINGRAY

MOUTH

Hammerheads have much smaller mouths than other kinds of sharks. Their front teeth are little but very sharp.

The teeth at the back of their mouths are large and flat. Hammerheads use them to mash up their food.

NOSE

A hammerhead's **nostrils** are set far apart on its wide nose. This helps the shark know which direction a smell is coming from.

NOSTRIL

AMPULLAE

The shark has another way to find prey. A hammerhead has small holes in the skin on its face called ampullae (AM-pull-ee). These help the predator sense things in the water.

EYES

EYE

A hammerhead shark's eyes are on the sides of its head. This lets the shark see all around.

The shark can see very well when there is not a lot of light. This is helpful when hunting deep underwater.

SKIN

Hammerhead sharks are covered in tiny pointed **scales**. These scales make their skin feel very rough.

Small **ridges** on the scales help send smells in the water to the shark's nostrils.

SKELETON

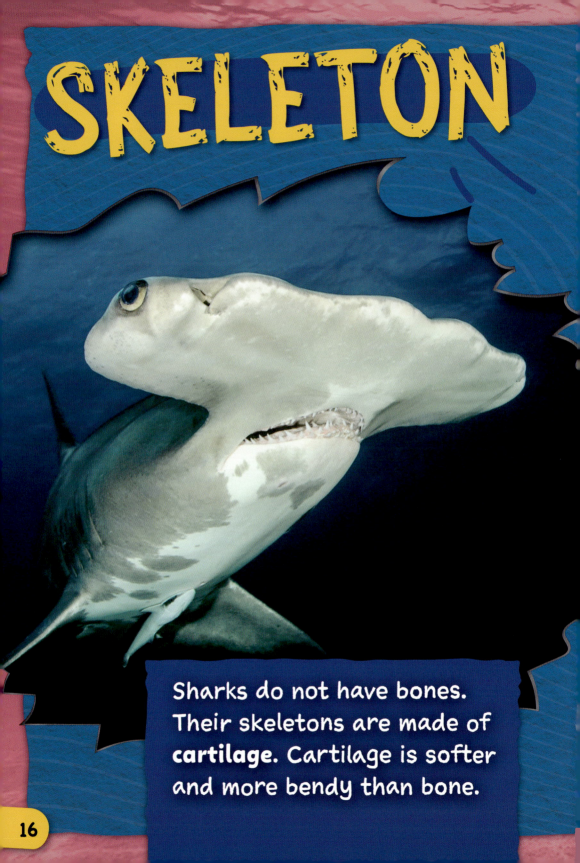

Sharks do not have bones. Their skeletons are made of **cartilage**. Cartilage is softer and more bendy than bone.

Because sharks can easily bend their bodies, they are able to turn more quickly than other types of fish. This makes them deadly predators.

FINS

Hammerhead sharks have a few kinds of fins. They are most well known for the tall dorsal fins on their backs.

DORSAL FIN

Sometimes, hammerheads roll to the side. Then, they use their dorsal fin to help them move up and down more easily.

TAIL

Hammerhead sharks also have tall tails. They move their tails side to side when they swim. This pushes them forward.

These predators swim slowly while they look for food. They speed up when they spot their prey.

LIFE CYCLE

Baby hammerhead sharks are called pups. They grow inside their mother's body. Some types of hammerheads have rounder heads when they are born.

These pups are on their own as soon as they are born. Hammerhead sharks can live for about 30 years.

GLOSSARY

cartilage the strong, rubbery stuff that makes up a shark's skeleton

nostrils two openings in a nose used for smelling

predators animals that hunt and eat other animals

prey an animal that is hunted and eaten by another animal

ridges parts that are slightly raised

scales small, hard pieces that form a shark's skin

INDEX

ampullae 11
cartilage 16
eyes 12
fins 18–19
nostrils 10, 15
pups 22–23
scales 14–15
tail 20
teeth 8–9, 14